Basics of SQL injection Analysis, Detection and Prevention

Jagdish Halde

Basics of SQL injection Analysis, Detection and Prevention

Web Security

LAP LAMBERT Academic Publishing

Impressum / Imprint
Bibliografische Information der Deutschen Nationalbibliothek: Die Deutsche
Nationalbibliothek verzeichnet diese Publikation in der Deutschen Nationalbibliografie;
detaillierte bibliografische Daten sind im Internet über http://dnb.d-nb.de abrufbar.
Alle in diesem Buch genannten Marken und Produktnamen unterliegen warenzeichen-,
marken- oder patentrechtlichem Schutz bzw. sind Warenzeichen oder eingetragene
Warenzeichen der jeweiligen Inhaber. Die Wiedergabe von Marken, Produktnamen,
Gebrauchsnamen, Handelsnamen, Warenbezeichnungen u.s.w. in diesem Werk berechtigt
auch ohne besondere Kennzeichnung nicht zu der Annahme, dass solche Namen im Sinne
der Warenzeichen- und Markenschutzgesetzgebung als frei zu betrachten wären und
daher von jedermann benutzt werden dürften.

Bibliographic information published by the Deutsche Nationalbibliothek: The Deutsche
Nationalbibliothek lists this publication in the Deutsche Nationalbibliografie; detailed
bibliographic data are available in the Internet at http://dnb.d-nb.de.
Any brand names and product names mentioned in this book are subject to trademark,
brand or patent protection and are trademarks or registered trademarks of their respective
holders. The use of brand names, product names, common names, trade names, product
descriptions etc. even without a particular marking in this works is in no way to be
construed to mean that such names may be regarded as unrestricted in respect of
trademark and brand protection legislation and could thus be used by anyone.

Coverbild / Cover image: www.ingimage.com

Verlag / Publisher:
LAP LAMBERT Academic Publishing
ist ein Imprint der / is a trademark of
OmniScriptum GmbH & Co. KG
Heinrich-Böcking-Str. 6-8, 66121 Saarbrücken, Deutschland / Germany
Email: info@lap-publishing.com

Herstellung: siehe letzte Seite /
Printed at: see last page
ISBN: 978-3-659-61224-4

Zugl. / Approved by: San Jose, San Jose State University, 2008

Copyright © 2014 OmniScriptum GmbH & Co. KG
Alle Rechte vorbehalten. / All rights reserved. Saarbrücken 2014

ABSTRACT

Web sites are databases, static sites, and most of the time a combination of both. Web sites need protection in their database to assure security. An SQL injection attacks interactive web applications that provide database services. These applications take user inputs and use them to create an SQL query at run time. In an SQL injection attack, an attacker might insert a malicious SQL query as input to perform an unauthorized database operation. Using SQL injection attacks, an attacker could retrieve or modify confidential and sensitive information from a database. It may jeopardize the confidentiality and security of Web sites which totally depends on databases. This report presents a "code reengineering" to implicitly protect applications written in PHP from SQL injection attacks and uses an original approach that combines static as well as dynamic analysis (Ettore Merlo, Dominic Letarte, Giuliano Antoniol, 2007). In this report, I mentioned an automated technique for moving out SQL injection vulnerabilities from Java code by converting plain text inputs received from users into prepared statements (Stephen Thomas and Laurie Williams, 2007).

ACKNOWLEDGEMENTS

I thank my advisor, Dr. Robert Chun, whose guidance, support, and dedication is priceless. Dr. Chun is an educator in the truest sense of the word. I especially thank to IEEE (Institute of Electrical and Electronics Engineers, Inc.) for providing recent information about my topic.

It has been a challenging, yet rewarding journey which I could not have completed alone and am grateful for your support.

Thank you.

Table of Contents

List of Figures

1.0. Introduction

In recent years, widespread adoption of the internet has resulted in rapid advances in information technologies. The internet is used by the general population for purposes such as financial transactions, educational endeavors, and countless other activities. The use of the internet for accomplishing important tasks, such as transferring a balance from a bank account, always comes with a security risk. Today's web sites strive to keep their users' data confidential and after years of doing secure business online, these companies have become experts in information security. The database systems behind these secure websites store non-critical data along with sensitive information, in a way that allows the information owners quick access while blocking break-in attempts from unauthorized users.

A common break-in strategy is to try to access sensitive information from a database by first generating a query that will cause the database parser to malfunction, followed by applying this query to the desired database. Such an approach to gaining access to private information is called SQL injection. Since databases are everywhere and are accessible from the internet, dealing with SQL injection has become more important than ever. Although current database systems have little vulnerability, the Computer Security Institute discovered that every year about 50% of databases experience at least one security breach. The loss of revenue associated with such breaches has been estimated to be over four million dollars. Additionally, recent research by the "Imperva Application

Defence Center" concluded that at least 92% of web applications are susceptible to "malicious attack" (Ke Wei, M. Muthuprasanna, Suraj Kothari, 2007).

To get a better understanding of SQL injection, we need to have a good understanding of the kinds of communications that take place during a typical session between a user and a web application. The following figure shows the typical communication exchange between all the components in a typical web application system.

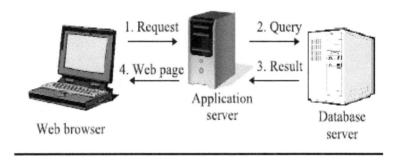

Figure 1: "Web application Architecture "
Source: Gary Wassermann Zhendong Su, Sound and Precise Analysis of Web Applications for Injection Vulnerabilities, University of California, Davis, 2007

A web application, based on the above model, takes text as input from users to retrieve information from a database. Some web applications assume that the input is legitimate and use it to build SQL queries to access a database. Since these web applications do not validate user queries before submitting them to retrieve data, they become more susceptible to SQL injection attacks. For example, attackers, posing as normal users, use maliciously crafted input text containing SQL instructions to produce SQL queries on the web application end. Once processed by the web application, the accepted malicious query may break the security policies of the underlying database architecture because the result of the query might cause the database parser to malfunction and release sensitive information.

The goal of this project is to build an automated fix generation method to prevent SQL injection vulnerability from plain text SQL statements. In an automated method approach, a server will gather information about previously known vulnerabilities, specifically SQL statements, generate a patch, and apply patch. The process can be completed by someone with no security expertise and secure legacy code, which will allow developers to fix the SQL injection vulnerability.

2.0 Related Work

I reviewed a number of electronic journal articles from IEEE journals and from ACM, and gathered some information from web sites to gain sufficient knowledge about SQL injection attacks. Following are the papers from which I covered different important strategies to prevent SQL injection attacks.

1. From "Using Parse Tree Validation to Prevent SQL Injection Attacks" ACM, I covered the techniques for sql injection discovery. This paper also covered very well the SQL parse tree validation that I mentioned in report (Gregory T. Buehrer, Bruce W. Weide, and Paolo A. G. Sivilotti, 2005)

2. From "The Essence of Command Injection Attacks in Web Applications" ACM, they covered the techniques to check and sanitize input query using SQLCHECK, it use the augmented queries and SQLCHECK grammar to validate query. (Zhendong Su and Gary Wassermann, 2006)

3. From "Using Automated Fix Generation to Secure SQL Statements" IEEE CNF, they covered brief background, SQL statement, and vulnerability replacement methods (Stephen Thomas and Laurie Williams, 2007).

4. From "Automated Protection of PHP Applications against SQL-injection Attacks" they covered an original method to protect application automatically from SQL injection attacks. The original approach combines static analysis, dynamic analysis, and automatic code re-engineering to secure existing properties (Ettore Merlo, Dominic Letarte, Giuliano Antoniol, 2007).

5. From "Preventing SQL Injection Attacks in Stored Procedures", they also provided a novel approach to shield the stored procedures from attack and detect SQL injection from it (Ke Wei, M. Muthuprasanna, Suraj Kothari, 2007). This method combines runtime check with static application code analysis so that they can eliminate vulnerability to attack. The key behind this attack is that it alters the structure of the original SQL statement and identifies the SQL injection attack. The method is divided in two phases, one is offline and another one is runtime. In the offline phase, stored procedures use a parser to pre-process and detect SQL statements in the execution call for runtime analysis. In the runtime phase, the technique controlled all runtime generated SQL queries related with the user input and checks these with the original structure of the SQL

8

statement after getting input from the user. Once this technique detects the malicious SQL statements it prevents the access of these statements to the database and provides details about attack.

2.1 SQL Injection Discovery Technique:

It is not compulsory for an attacker to visit the web pages using a browser to find if SQL injection is possible on the site. Generally attackers build a web crawler to collect all URLs available on each and every web page of the site. Web crawler is also used to insert illegal characters into the query string of a URL and check for any error result sent by the server. If the server sends any error message as a result, it is a strong positive indication that the illegal special meta character will pass as a part of the SQL query, and hence the site is open to SQL Injection attack. For example Microsoft Internet Information Server by default shows an ODBC error message if an any meta character or an unescaped single quote is passed to SQL Server. The Web crawler only searches the response text for the ODBC messages.

2.2 SQL PARSE TREE VALIDATION:

A Parse tree is nothing but the data structure built by the developer for the parsed representation of a statement. To parse the statement, the grammar of that parse statement's language is needed. In this method, by parsing two statements and comparing their parse trees, we can check if the two queries are equal. When attacker successfully injects SQL into a database query, the parse tree of the intended SQL query and the resulting SQL query generated after attacker input do not match. The following figure shows the representation of a parse tree. [4]

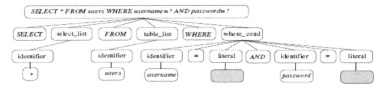

Figure 2: A SELECT query with two user inputs

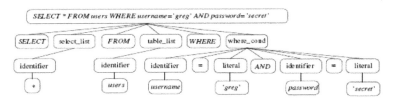

Figure 3: The same SELECT query as in Figure 1, with the user input inserted

In the above parse tree the programmer-supplied portion is hard-coded, and the user-supplied portion is represented as a vacant leaf node in the above parse tree. A leaf node must be the value of a literal, and it must be in the position where vacant space is located. The SQL query for the above parse tree is as below.

SELECT * FROM users WHERE username=? AND password=?.

The question marks are place holders for input leaf nodes. [4]

10

2.3 Approach for SQL CHECK:

```
<%!
// database connection info
String dbDriver = "com.mysql.jdbc.Driver";
String strConn = "jdbc:mysql://"
    + "sport4sale.com/sport";
String dbUser = "manager";
String dbPassword = "athltpass";
// generate query to send
String sanitizedName =
replace(request.getParameter("name"),"'","''");
String sanitizedCardType =
replace(request.getParameter("cardtype"),
    "'","''");
String query = "SELECT cardnum FROM accounts"
    + " WHERE uname='" + sanitizedName + "'"
    + " AND cardtype=" + sanitizedCardType + ";";
try {// connect to database and send query
    java.sql.DriverManager.registerDriver(
        (java.sql.Driver)
    (Class.forName(dbDriver).newInstance()));
    javaq.sql.Connection conn =
    java.sql.DriverManager.getConnecion(
        strConn, dbUser, dbPassword);
    java.sql.Statement stmt =
    conn.createStatement();
    java.sql.ResultSet rs =
    stmt.executeQuery(query);
    // generate html output
out.println("<html><body><table>");
while(rs.next()) {out.println("<tr> <td>");
    out.println(rs.getString(1));
    out.println("</td> </tr>");
    }if (rs != null) {rs.close();
}out.println("</table> </body> </html>");
    } catch (Exception e)
{ out.println(e.toString()); } %>
```

Figure 4: A JSP page for retrieving credit card numbers.

Web applications have SQL injection vulnerabilities because they do not sanitize the inputs they use to construct structured output. Consider the snippet shown in Figure 4. The code is for an online store. The website provides user input field to allow the user to keep their credit card information which user can use for future purchases. **Replace** method is used to escape the quotes so that any single quote characters in the input is considered as a literal and not a string delimiters. Replace method is intended to block

11

attacks by preventing an attacker from ending the string and adding SQL injection code. Although, **cardtype** is a numeric column, if an attacker passes 2 OR 1=1" as the card type, all account numbers in the database will be returned and displayed. [5]

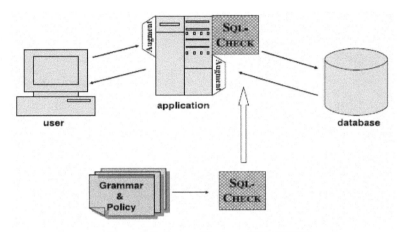

Figure 5. System architecture of SQLCHECK.

In this approach they track through the program, the substrings receive from user input and sanitize that substrings syntactically. The aim behind this program is to block the queries in which the input substrings changes the syntactic structure of the rest of the query. They use the meta-data to watch user's input, displayed as '_' and '_,' to mark the end and beginning of the each user input string. This meta-data pass the string through an assignments, and concatenations, so that when a query is ready to be sent to the database, it has a matching pairs of markers that identify the substring from the input. These annotated queries called an augmented query. To build a parser for the augmented grammar and attempt to parse each augmented query Steve [5] use a parse generator.

12

Query meets the syntactic constraints and considered legitimate if it parses successfully. Else, it fails the syntactic constraints and interprets it as an SQL injection attack.

Figure-5 shows the system architecture of the checking system. Grammar of the output language is used to build SQLCHECK and a policy mentioned permitted syntactic forms, it resides on the web server and taps generated queries. In spite of the input's source, each input which is to be passed into some query, gets augmented with the meta-characters '_' and '_'. Finally application creates augmented queries, which SQLCHEKCK attempts to parse, and if a query parses successfully, SQLCHECK sends it the meta-data to the database, else the query get rejected.

3.0 Background for SQL Statement

This section gives a brief idea about the SQL injection vulnerability and a related SQL injection attacks. SQL injection vulnerability means the combination of dynamic SQL statement compilation and a weak in input validation. This input validation forces input to change the structure of a SQL query. Such combinations are generally found in java. Following example shows the code that initially have plain text SQL statement which dynamically produces the SQL query based on a variable input (userISBN). Moreover, without any input verification it creates the SQL query with use of string concatenation.

```
"Statement stmt ="
"conn.createStatement();"
"ResultSet rs ="
"stmt.executeQuery("select amount from"
"books where isbn = '" + userISBN + "'");"
```

13

In this example, by using known keywords from SQL statement, attacker maliciously tries to update sensitive information in databases. Here attacker tries to change the structure of the execution query that system does not allow. Attacker could give the malicious input values of 111' OR '1'='1 for user ISBN. The extra "appended OR '1'='1 clause" turns an entire where clause always true and as a result the query opens up the SQL statement to fetch and send all results without articulating which result is supposed to be send to the user. The attack get success because of OR '1'='1 clause which set the value of where clause true in all conditions. [5]

3.1 SQL Statements

Two types of SQL statements are used to prevent SQL injection attack.

3.1.1 Prepared statements

The statements that have been pre-complied with the SQL query called as prepared statement. SQL query is nothing but the plain text representation of the statement written by programmer while developing database access programmer. Prepared statements in SQL query has bind variables that allow you to put inputs into subsequent queries. In Java input set method is used to set bind variable such as setString(index, output) call for a String type output variable. Set methods render the additional security to confirm each input variable with respect to its declared type. The primary purpose of prepared statement is to increase security and efficiency. Prepared statements are built to execute same statement number of times while compiling statement. This property is not

14

available in plain text SQL statement. The functionality of the prepared function is same as the plain text SQL statements, but the prepared statements have more structured way than the plain text SQL statements. Manipulation of the structure of the pre-complied query can prevent using structure handling of the prepared statement, hence preclude SQL injection vulnerability.

The limitation of the prepared statement is they can only be created if the structure of the statement is known before the creation of the statement. Thus the dynamically created statements on input for a part of the structure are not to be prepared statements. Prepared statements are precompiled once the statements are built by the Connection object in Java. When all of the inputs are set into the statement and the statement is executed, it sent to the database. [7]

3.1.2 Run time automated Statement

The benefit of automated statement is that it checks for vulnerability of SQL queries dynamically at run time. This method not totally depend on the prepared statement, it validate the SQL code by putting constraints on run time environment to avoid malicious SQL statement. In this method the proposed solution to avoid an SQL injection attack is, by analyzing the parse tree of the SQL statement, creating the custom validation code, and packaging the susceptible statement in the validation code (Stephen Thomas and Laurie Williams, 2007). In the run time automated statement Stephen Thomas uses parse trees in a dynamic way to make the comparison at run time to find out whether two queries are functionally identical. The parse tree helps to find out the structure and the input variables for SQL statement. [9]

4.0 Vulnerability Reinstatement

To achieve perfect secrecy, we either append the secured SQL statement to the vulnerable statement or reinstate the whole vulnerable statement. If the database Connection object is out of scope of execution call then the vulnerable statements are in a method signature. If the vulnerable statement is in the state of any detectable signature method then we does not require replacing of the statement. In some cases, if we change the statements, then we have to change the API too. We can achieve secrecy without changing or modifying the statement creation code, but to eliminate redundancy in object we require complete replacement of the plain text SQL statements. In above cases, we will replace the execution call as

PreparedStatement preparedStmt = Statement.getConnection().prepareStatement(ps SQL); this is the prepared statement formation call.

Statement: Actual Statement objects in Java code.

PSsql: Generated SQL query with bind variables.

The formation call helps to prevent SQL injection attack by bypassing the Statement and create the secure "Prepared Statement- based on the SQL statement". In this way we can achieve the perfect secrecy, prevent the SQL injection vulnerability, and the SQL injection attack. [11]

16

4.1 Model-based guard constructor prevention approach

Model-based guard constructor prevention is an efficient method in preventing an SQL injection attack. This method is established on breaking the suitable conjunction of input, code, data, and database access situation that would employ an SQL injection attack. Spontaneously inserting appropriate guards before allowing access to the database, we can avoid an SQL injection attack. As shown in the Figure-6, initially instrument the PHP string to collect samples of query which authentically used at database application program interface call point. These queries called as a set of trusted test cases. From flow of diagram we can easily understand the prevention of an SQL injection attack. Instrumentation is nothing but to add an output instruction before database application interface calls, as below.

Sql_query(... Expression...);

After passing this expression thorough automated approach it becomes:

```
$string = Expression;
fRead($file handle; $string));
$result = sql_query($ string);
```

After running the trusted test cases to gather the plain text strings that are produced dynamically at various call sites matching to trusted queries. It is a straightforward to create model guards from sets of ASTs leading to legitimate queries. Justifiable queries are parsed by automated approach and corresponding "ASTs" is stored for every call site. To avoid generalization between queries "ASTs" are stored independently. [13]

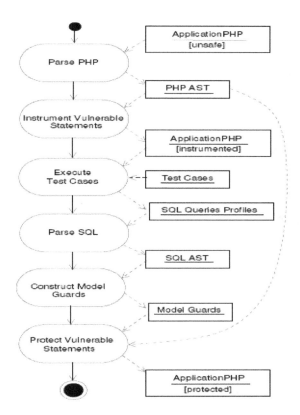

Figure 6: "Automated Protection"
Source: Ettore Merlo, Dominic Letarte, Giuliano Antoniol, SQL injection attack
recognition and SQL-FSM contravention, 2007.

ASTs are generalized by type rather than image, because constants, strings and

additional types of data are also stored in the ASTs. On the other hand, application

dependent identifiers, such as the names of the tables, number of columns, and rows, are

counted as a part of syntactic structure of the SQL query which plays crucial role to prevent malicious substitution of table or column names in the valid queries. Therefore this method permits number of queries with same syntactic structure, but with different values of data. Using special call site, model guard invokes the SQL parser on the database where we are working currently to and obtains the matching SQL AST. The formed "AST" is compare with the stored valid "ASTs" for the same call site. If the match points towards positive result then the current query has a compatible syntactic structure with the valid query from the trusted set. Only positively equivalent queries are allowed to be processed to the database application programming interface, and all other queries are get rejected. In this way we prevent the access to the database from crafted malicious queries.

Generally "ASTs" are stored as images, but it stored as token strings containing token types where an application table names and field names have become keywords. Tables' names have been stored as identifier token types in local configuration. In the subsequent section, these token strings called as reference patterns.

An example of trusted query is as below. In this example snooping call at line 333 in file browse.php is as below.

"SELECT post id"
"FROM phptb240t posts"
"WHERE"
"Poster_id = 5"

Where phptb240 posts is a configuration dependent local table names. Poster id is field names set in application logic.

And reference patterns related to the formerly shown query is as below:

browse:php : 240
"SELECT POST ID"

19

"FROM SQL ID"
"WHERE"
"POSTER ID OP EQUAL INTEGER LITERAL"
(Ettore Merlo, Dominic Letarte, Giuliano Antoniol, 2007)

From above example, we can observe that phptb240 posts discerned as an identifier, and poster id is supposed as keywords of the application. Because of same syntactic structure of a valid query, and changing field names with confidential ones, we must prevent SQL injection attacks. Post id and poster id in above example can be accessed in any local configuration of phptb, but they won't be replaced by other field. Same as above poster identifier value only be replace by integer value. Susceptible SQL query statement can be make secure by substituting them with model-based guards that execute the appropriate checks at every call site and allow an access to the appropriate database application programming interface while successful checks. We required model-based guards and the re-engineering of source code to change call from mySql to the model-based guards". Figure-7 shows an example of the model-based guard written in Java.

```
class sqlModelCheckerCl {

    staticHashSetmodel = newHashSet();

    public static void init() {
        // initialize model checker
        // with all reference patterns
        ...
        model.add("search.php : 221 SELECT ...");
        ...
    }

    String parseQuery(String query) {
        // SQL parser implementation
    }

    bool sqlModelGuard(String callSite,
                       String query) {
        if (model.contains(callSite +
            parseQuery(query))) {
            mysql(query);
        } else {
            System.exit(1);
        }
    }
}
```

Figure 7: Conceptual example of model guard in Java.
Source: Ettore Merlo, Dominic Letarte, Giuliano Antoniol, SQL injection attack
recognition and SQL-FSM contravention, 2007.

Giving proper call to the model-based guard, we can protect the application from an
SQL injection attack. Model guard construction is equivalent to the average length of the
SQL queries executed in the test, and number of test cases. In this paper : Ettore Merlo,

Dominic Letarte, and Giuliano Antoniol used automated construction process for the model-guards which is very simple and have an enough scope to make this mode more complicated to increase power of the parsing queries. Model-base guard is much better than the fixed form per call site method. Model-guard build automatically depends on the dynamic approximation for security specification. Small number of legitimate queries at a call site also affects the efficiency of automation. This approach provides a feasible amount of protection from an SQL injection attack. [13]

4.2 Preventing SQL injection method

Stephen Thomas and Laurie Williams explained in detail about the methods which are used to prevent an SQL injection attacks. [2]

1) Static analysis

2) Run time analysis

These techniques are based on the stored procedures, Authors' used control flow graph that notifies what user inputs to the dynamic built SQL statement. Control flow graphs are very useful to minimize the set of SQL statements to verify users input. In run time analysis we access information about stored statement from Finite State Automaton to narrow the verification procedure and to indicate the user's inputs true or false. [2]

4.3 Static analyses of stored procedure

In static analysis authors provides parser called stored procedure parser which is used to extracts the "control flow graph" from the saved procedures, we can see in detailed about the control graph in following section. At the start we label every execution statement in the control flow graph and then use the backtracking method to verify all statements participated in the formation of the SQL statement in the control flow graph. In the SQL graph, a statements which are depend on user's input are screened and flags are set on it to monitor their behavior at run time. In this method, using Finite State Automaton we compare the statement with dynamically created SQL statement of user inputs with the original SQL statement. The statement created by users input which tries to change the original pattern of the parser will indicated by flag as dangerous statement and provide the related information. More than one execution statement may be possible for single "stored procedure" statement. There are different kinds of procedure statements available, and only the statements which accept input from user are vulnerable to an SQL injection attack. Now using SQL control graph we try to optimize the query that need to process dynamically in order to provide validity. Following figure gives a clear understanding of static analysis. Four different SQL queries Q1, Q2, Q3, and Q4 are in the stored procedure shown as nodes within a boundary displayed in dotted circle. I1, I2, and, I3 are the three different inputs received from users which are from outside of the logical boundaries. Suppose a user enter the input I in the SQL query Q and the relationship between input I and query Q is represented by R. D represents the dependencies in SQL diagram that link the one SQL query to another. The user input I

23

accepted by previous query is transfers to another query through the dependency link. In SQL queries one of these nodes is selected as a representative query and it consider a start point to point other queries. Dependency in the figure is shown by directed arrows. [2]

Q_1, Q_2, Q_3, Q_4 I_1, I_2, I_3	SQL Queries User Inputs
R_1	$I_1 \in Q_1$
R_2	$I_2 \in Q_1$
R_3	$I_1 \in Q_3$
R_4	$I_2 \in Q_2$
R_5	$I_3 \in Q_4$
D_1	$Q_3 \subset Q_1$
D_2	$Q_2 \subset Q_1$

Figure 8: SQL- control graph
Source: Ke Wei, M. Muthuprasanna, Suraj Kothari, Preventing SQL injection attacks in stored procedures, 2007.

4.4 Advantages of static analysis

1) SQL graph representation used to reduce the runtime scanning overhead of program by preventing the number of queries that are not required to execute in stored procedure.

2) SQL control graph does not include the query which not takes an input from user.

3) The queries which includes input from user to access the database information are counted towards SQL control graph representation.

4.5 Dynamic analysis

In dynamic analysis, SQL injection attack checker function is used to categorize the user input. In this method, author used "current session" identifier to identify the input taken from user, and using same session id, builds a finite state automaton. Figure 5 shows the finite state automaton that accepts inputs from user. To check legitimacy of SQL statement received from user, the SQL statement along with user inputs is compared with corresponding SQL statement of finite state automaton. If the SQL queries generated at run time using user input is not satisfy the semantics of the intended SQL queries in the FSA (Finite State Automata) then these SQL queries are set as SQL injection attack otherwise these queries should passed to the database access.

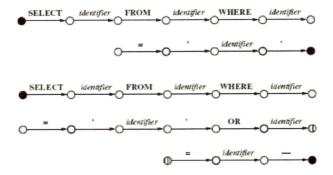

Figure 9: SQL Injection Attack Recognition and SQL-FSM Contravention

Hence, we can easily obviate the crafted malicious queries and only permits the legitimate queries to access databases. Due to use of finite state automata this method achieves perfect secrecy to screen the legitimate queries. [12]

5.0 SQLiX – Sql Injection Scanner:

5.1 SQLiX before enhancement:

SQLiX Scanner can be found at the Open Web Application Security Project (OWASP) site. OWASP is a worldwide free and open community focused on improving the security of application software. SQLiX is coded in Perl, able to crawl, detect an SQL injection and identify the back-end database vulnerability. SQLiX uses various Perl modules from CPAN- CPAN is nothing but the Comprehensive Perl Archive Network. On CPAN you can find large amount of Perl software and their documentation, so that any coder can use this library and Perl module in their projects. We will see in more detail about the Perl modules which are used by SQLiX in Perl module section.

Following are the methods which are used in the original SQLiX:

1)   Error Generation: Error generation method is a very simple and is typically depends on meta characters like single quotes and double quotes.

2)   Method blind injection: In Blind SQL injection methods, the web application which are vulnerable to SQL injection are not visible to an attacker. These attacks are display differently depending up on the results of a logical statement injected in to the database

3)   Statement injection: From the following example you can get clear understanding about the statement injection method.

The original URL:

26

0) is http:// localhost/acu/indexacu.php/news.php?id=25.

SQLiX will try to compare the html content of the original request with the following Urls.

i)   http://localhost/acu/indexacu.php/news.php?id=25%20or%201=1

ii) http://localhost/acu/indexacu.php/news.php?id=25%20or%201=0

if the URL i) is provides the same result as a http request 0) and URL ii) does not, the SQLiX will conclude that SQL injection is possible on the given URL.

Also SQLiX uses multiple methods to determine if the current server-side script is vulnerable to SQL injection.

1)   Conditional errors injection.

2)   Blind injection based on integers, strings or statements.

3)   MS-SQL verbose error messages.

4)   It also able to recognize version of database.

SQLiX has three main APIs which are helps to build the various types of SQL attacks. And it has SQLiX.pl is the main file which handles and used to invoke these APIs on every stacked URL.

From following example you can get clear understanding of the command line usage

Perl SQLiX.pl -crawl="http://test.acunetix.com" -exploit -
method_taggy -v=5

27

5.2 Perl Modules Used in SQLiX:

Crawl is the target specification which takes the given URL as a main URL and crawl through all the web pages and forms available under that URL. The crawl target specification uses Perl module to crawl.

The crawler needs **Spider.pm** Perl module to spider through entire web site and collects all URL available on the every pages and stack in the array for further operation. To fetch URL from the pages and forms, SQLiX uses the **Mechaniz.pm** Perl module. It is the heart of the tool that plays the crucial role to collect URL for further process. SQLiX use **Checksite.pm** module to check and validate the URL available on the each web page of that site. It first validates the URL and then only stacks it for the further SQL injection operation. The Spider uses the robot rules mechanism. This means that it will always get the /robots.txt file from the root of the web server to see if we are allowed (actually "not disallowed") to access pages as a robot. Spider uses the RobotRule.pm to read the robot.txt file available on server and according the rules it accesses the URLs on the site. If owner of the site restrict to crawl some URLs from his site then the owner must write this URLs in robot.txt file and so nobody can crawl these URLs. That rule is followed by the all crawler developer.

SQLiX have very interesting and important feature rather than other scanners is of building your own function. You can build your own function to inject malicious code into the database and test for different vulnerabilities. This feature is not available in any other vulnerability scanners available in market. Also instead of giving main URL in command line interface for crawl, you can list the number of Main URLs which you wish to crawl in one file and call that file.

Exploit option is used to attack one of the vulnerabilities which were found in the injection attack and will try to extract information. By default shows the version of the database.

V is the option used to display the debug message and information about the vulnerabilities. It has different value of verbosity for minimum information display and maximum debug information about the all URLs from 0 to 5.

Here is the output of the SQLiX using command line interface:

```
C:\SQLiX\SQLiX_v1.0>
C:\SQLiX\SQLiX_v1.0>perl SQLiX.pl -crawl="http://test.acunetix.com" -all -exploit -v=2
=====================================================================
                    -- SQLiX --
 ⌐ Copyright 2006 Cedric COCHIN, All Rights Reserved.
=====================================================================

Analysing URI obtained by crawling [http://test.acunetix.com]
   http://test.acunetix.com/
   http://test.acunetix.com/privacy.php
   http://test.acunetix.com/userinfo.php
   http://test.acunetix.com/login.php
   http://test.acunetix.com/signup.php
   http://test.acunetix.com/AJAX/index.php
   http://test.acunetix.com/guestbook.php
   http://test.acunetix.com/cart.php
   http://test.acunetix.com/disclaimer.php
   http://test.acunetix.com/artists.php
   http://test.acunetix.com/comment.php?aid=3
        [+] working on aid
               [+] Method: MS-SQL error message
               [+] Method: SQL error message
               [+] Method: MySQL comment injection
                      [ERROR] Parameter doesn't impact content
               [+] Method: SQL Blind String Injection
                      [ERROR] Parameter doesn't impact content
   http://test.acunetix.com/artists.php?artist=3
        [+] working on artist
               [+] Method: MS-SQL error message
               [+] Method: SQL error message
               [+] Method: MySQL comment injection
                      [FOUND] MySQL Comment based injection (integer based)
                      [FOUND] MySQL comment injection
   http://test.acunetix.com/listproducts.php?artist=3
        [+] working on artist
               [+] Method: MS-SQL error message
               [+] Method: SQL error message
                      [WARNING] Match found in reference(NULL) - You have an
error in your SQL syntax
                      [INFO] Error with quote
```

```
                    [INFO] Current function: version()
                    [INFO] length: 255

                    [FOUND] SQL error message
   http://test.acunetix.com/comment.php?aid=2
           [+] working on aid
                    [+] Method: SQL Blind Integer Injection
                            [ERROR] Parameter doesn't impact content
                    [+] Method: SQL Blind Statement Injection
                            [ERROR] Parameter doesn't impact content
                    [+] Method: SQL Blind String Injection
                            [ERROR] Parameter doesn't impact content

RESULTS:
The variable [artist] from [http://test.acunetix.com/artists.php?artist=3] is vu
lnerable to SQL Injection [Comment without quotes - MySQL].
The variable [artist] from [http://test.acunetix.com/listproducts.php?artist=3]
is vulnerable to SQL Injection [Error message (NULL) - MySQL].
The variable [pic] from [http://test.acunetix.com/product.php?pic=7] is vulnerab
le to SQL Injection [Comment without quotes - MySQL].
The variable [cat] from [http://test.acunetix.com/listproducts.php?cat=4] is vul
nerable to SQL Injection [Error message (NULL) - MySQL].
```

From output you can get idea that how SQLiX collect the all URLs from the web site and

detect vulnerable URLs which are susceptible for SQL Injection attack.

6.0   Enhancements in SQLiX:

6.1 What I achieved?

Three major challenging enhancements that I am completed successfully in this project

i)   Enhance the crawler to handle HTTP post and fills a forms automatically.

ii)   Created Graphical User Interface (GUI) for SQLiX.

iii)   Added a Module to Detect Cross Site Scripting (XSS) attacks.

6.2 SQLiX HTTP Post Method and fill form automatically:

Enhance the crawler to handle HTTP Post Method and fill the forms available on the webpage is one of the toughest and critical mile stone in my project. This enhancement made the SQLiX more powerful than earlier one.

6.2.1 Working:

After enhancement, crawler is able to handle the HTTP Post method request. Crawler also able to detects and fills the forms available on the current web page. After detecting the forms on the current web page, my code checks the input type, name of input type and type of input type of every field of the form. In next step my code fills the dummy data in each field of the form according to their type. Once it done with filling the dummy data in a form the $response = $ua->request($form->click) function submit the data in database and generates the content. Content is nothing but the link created from form's all field name and dummy data corresponding to it. Finally in the last step my code passes this content to the main SQLiX .pl program to make different combination of the original URL for that particular form. Now injection step get start and control will hand over to the all different method which inject all combination of URLs in to the database to get some unauthorized information. Now the power of SQLiX of injecting number of injection in the database is increased drastically, because it applying injection method for each and every field of form instead of applies only on main URL.

To implement this module I used following CPAN Perl modules.

i)   LWP user agent

ii)   Html::parse

31

iii)   Html::Form

LWP user agent is the Perl module used to implement user agent. Actually UserAgent is the class and I am using its objects to dispatch web request. Basically, in general application creates an LWP::UserAgent object, and then configures that object with parameters, then it create an instance of HTTP::Request for the request the needs to be performed. This request is then passed to one of the request method of the UserAgent. UserAgent then get back to you in the form of HTTP::Response object. There are three convenient methods for sending and receiving common requests: GET ( ), POST ( ) and HEAD ( ). These methods do the creation of the request object hidden. To feel every communication as http style this library constructs HTTP::Request object and HTTP::Response object even for non-HTTP resource.

The following constructor methods are available to create object:

$ua = LWP::UserAgent->new (%options)

This method constructs a new LWP::UserAgent object and returns it. You need to provide key/value pair arguments to set up the initial state. Now $ua is the handler for the object of LWP::UserAgent.

6.2.2 HTML Parser:

HTML Parser module is used to create object that will recognize and differentiate the markup and plain text in the html documents. The objects of this class recognize the different kinds of markup and text and invoke the corresponding event handlers. The document that you need to pass can be passed in arbitrary chunks. I will pass the URLs which are stacked by the crawler. And the parse the given URL   and   separate   the

32

markup and text from html. After the it stack the all markup in local array that array we gone use for the next Perl module that is HTML Form.

6.2.3 HTML Form:

The object of HTML Form class has a single instance i.e. HTML<form>...</form>. Generally form consists of number of input types that usually have names, and which can have a various attributes and values. The state of a form can be pull off and then called to provide HTTP::Request object which can be passed to the method called request() of LWP::UserAgent. Following are the methods available:

@forms = HTML::Form->parse($response)

@forms = HTML::Form->parse($html_document, $base)

@forms = HTML::Form->parse($html_document, %opt)

An HTML document will parse and create HTML::Form objects for every form element vailable in that document using paser() class method. If you called this method in scalar context only returns the first form, and return empty list there is no form found. The variable $base is used as URI to retrieve the $html_document. If you retrieve this document using LWP then this parameter of HTML::Form obtained from the $response->bas() method shown as above.

Here is the little snippet that I used to retrieve content of the forms.

```
use LWP::UserAgent;
use HTML::Form;

    my $ua = LWP::UserAgent->new;
    my $response = $ua->get("http://www.tizag.com/htmlT/forms.php");
        #my $response = $ua->get("http://localhost/form.php");
    my @forms = HTML::Form->parse($response);
    foreach (@forms)
```

33

```
{
  my $form = $_;
      print stdout "Form :";
      print stdout "\n";
      my @inputs = $form->inputs;
      foreach (@inputs)
      {
        my $input = $_;
        print STDOUT $input->type;
        print " : " , $input->name;
        print stdout "\n";
      }
      print stdout "\n";
      print stdout "\n";
}
```

7.0 SQLiX GUI:

SQLiX had no GUI; the user had to remember all the option. As it has long list of options, it is very cumbersome if you have to attack a site with maximum set.

For the file option to specify the target URL, the user can directly select file from File Chooser Dialog. Through the GUI user can select the options directly. The output of the attack can be saved to a specified file. Below are the snap-shots of the application.

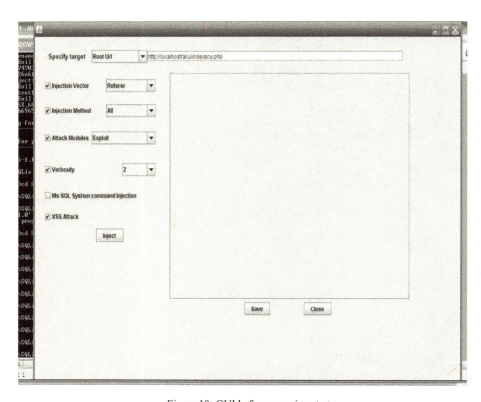

Figure 10: GUI before scanning starts

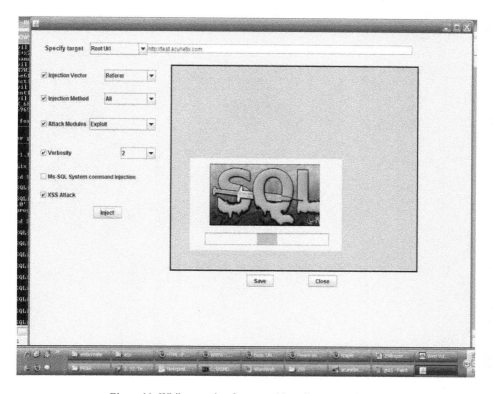

Figure 11: While scanning for root url http://test.acunetix.com.

From above screen shot it is clear that new user doesn't need to remember any option. And he can do different kind of testing by selecting various options from the GUI interface. Progress bar show the status of scanning which is not able to predict in command line.

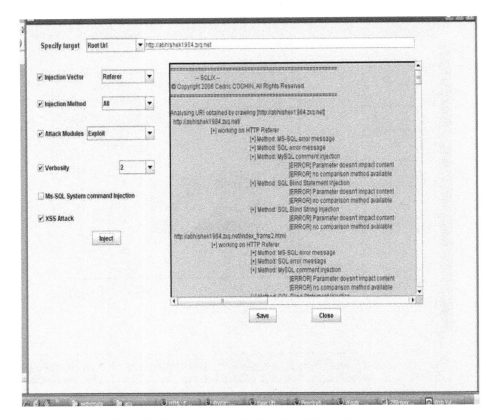

Figure 12: After Scan result will show in right hand side window.

8.0   Cross Site Scripting (XSS):

Cross Site Scripting is one of the most common application layer attacks. XSS targets the scripts, which are part of web page and are executed on the Clint-side instead server-side. Cross-site scripting attacks can occur wherever a user has the ability to publish content to a trusted web site. A malicious user can craft a client-side script, which performs some activity such as sending all sensitive information available on current browser to the particular email address. If this script seems to be legitimate and input is unchecked, this script will be loaded and run by each user visiting the web site. Attacker can do different kinds of attacks using XSS. Such as running "Active X" control from sites that is thought as trustworthy.   Attacker can also submit the XSS script which attracts the user attention. Attackers use the scripts which such as below.

```
<form> action="logoninformation.jsp" method="post"
    onsubmit="hackImg=new Image;
hackImg.src='http://www.malicioussite.com/'+document.forms(1).login.val
ue'+':'+ document.forms(1).password.value;"
</form>
```

This script is used to steal login information of the user.

Attacker inserts the script on the web site and when any attracted user hits the link , the script gets executed and sends login information of the site targeted in the script.

Now the attacker has to go of the targeted site for retrieving the login information. [17]

8.1 Type of XSS:

There are two major types of XSS.

i) **Non-permanent XSS**: For non-permanent SXX attacks require a user to visit a link which attracted user's attention and are crafted with malicious code. Upon visiting such links, the code inserted in the URL will be print and executed on the victim's web browser.

ii) **Permanent XSS**: This kind of XSS also called as stored vulnerability, and it is more dangerous then non-permanent XSS. In permanent XSS first the data provided by user is stored on server permanently, and the malicious user stored the malicious scripting code on server. Generally they stored such kind of data through comment form or suggestion form. And when the normal user search for other user's opinion about particular issue and if the malicious script gets retrieved from the server then it gets executed on attacker's web browser. And depending on the intensity of script it affects your computer. [19]

8.2 What I did in SQLiX to detect XSS Vulnerabilities:

To detect the XSS from the given web site we added the two functions to the SQLiX that are as below:

i)   SET XSS

ii) ATTACK XSS

SET XSS function is use to take the stack of URLs from the buffer and just hand over to the Attack XSS function. Attack XSS function is important function which uses the payload and tries different attacks on the list of URLS. If any one of the test case from the payload get succeed then the given URL is vulnerable to XSS.

8.3 How it works:

The script uses Web spider library to check the rules mentioned below.

The script scans the web pages and searches for scripts and forms where it can inject data.

The site is vulnerable for the following conditions

    i)   Checks whether a script allows http upload.

    ii)   When the return code is http 500

8.4 Small snippet of added code for the ATTACK XSS and explanation:

```
XSS Attack:
def attackXSS(self,page,dict):
        if dict=={}:
            err=""
            payload="<script>var SQLiX_"
            payload+=page.encode("hex_codec")
            payload+="_"

            payload+="QUERYSTRING".encode("hex_codec")
            payload+="=new Boolean();</script>"
            url=page+"?"+payload
            if url not in self.attackedGET:
              try:
                if self.verbose==2:
                    print "+ "+url
                 req = urllib2.Request(url)
                        u = urllib2.urlopen(req)
                data=u.read()
                    except (urllib2.URLError,socket.timeout),e:
                if hasattr(e,'code'):
                    data=""
                    else:
                    return
            if data.find(payload)>=0:
            {
                print "XSS (QUERY_STRING) in",page
                        print "\tEvil url:",url
```

40

```
}
            else:
    if u.code==500:
        print "500 HTTP Error code with"
        print "\tEvil url:",url
    self.attackedGET.append(url)
for k in dict.keys():
            err=""
  tmp=dict.copy()
  payload="<script>var SQLiX_"
  payload+=page.encode("hex_codec")
 payload+="_"
  payload+=k.encode("hex_codec")
  payload+="=new Boolean();</script>"
  tmp[k]=payload

 if data.find(payload)>=0:
        if self.color==0:
print "XSS ("+k+") in",page
        print "\tEvil url:",url
    else:
        print "XSS",":",url.replace(k+"=","\033[0;31m"+k+"\033[0;0m=")
            else:
    if u.code==500:
        print "500 HTTP Error code with"
        print "\tEvil url:",url
            self.attackedGET.append(url)
```

In above snippet AttackXss function which use the entire payload to check the available scripts in the given database and related to the given URL, and payload applies different test operation specified in payload. We just checking for the normal XSS and permanent XSS there are also different king of XSS can detect by improving the payload.

9.0   Other Commercial and Open source SQL injection scanners:

9.1 Acunetix web vulnerability scanner:

Acunetix scanner divides type of scanning according to the severity of the type of web attack. It divides in 4 type high, medium, low and informational severity. Acunetix is used to detect various types of web vulnerabilities as below.

i)   SQL injection

ii)   Cross site scripting

iii)   CGI scripting

iv)   Firewalls and SSL

v)   URL redirection

SQL injection and Cross site scripting scans are comes under the high severity type as they are considered most dangerous attacks in web security. Other attacks are categorized according to their severity on web services.

Although this scanner does little bit extra amount of scanning, it is very slow as compare to the other tool available in market and slower than SQLiX as well.

9.2 SQLmap:

Sqlmap is an SQL injection scanner build in Python. The aim of this tool is to detect SQL injection vulnerabilities and take advantage of these vulnerabilities on web application. Sqlmap initially detect the loop whole in you site and then use variety of option to perform extensive back-end database management, enumerate users, dump entire or specific DBMS, retrieve DBMS session user and database, read specific file on the file system etc. SQLmap is bit faster than acunetix web scanner but still slower than SQLiX, and it also make very few url injection in to the database as compare to SQLiX.

This tool also doesn't have GUI interface.

9.3 Wapiti:

Wapiti is command line based tool build in python and uses a Python library called lswww. This is the spider library helps to crawl each page on given web site. Wapiti allows us to inspect the security of our web site. This tool also used html Tidy lib to clean the html pages which are not will formatted. This library helps a lot lswww library to extract information from bad-coded html web pages. Basically it does black-box scans. Wapiti scans the all webpages available on you site and try to find out scripts and form where it can inject data to check how many types of attack are possible on selected injection point. Wapit can detect SQL injection and XSS (Cross Site Scripting) injection. Wapiti has one of the best features that it's able to differentiate temporary and permanent XSS vulnerabilities.

It does not provide a GUI interface and you must have to use it from command line interface. As this tool dosen't have GUI- interface I would like to give you a command line usage here.

Usage:

```
Wapiti-1.1.5 - A web application vulnerability scanner
Usage: python wapiti.py http://localhost/acu/indexacu.php [options]
Supported options are:
-s <url>
--start <url>
        To specify an url to start with
-x <url>
--exclude <url>
        To exclude an url from the scan (for example logout scripts)
        You can also use a wildcard (*)
        Exemple                        :                        -x
"http://localhost/acu/indexacu.php/?page=*&module=test"
        or -x http://server/base/admin/* to exclude a directory
-p <url_proxy>
--proxy <url_proxy>
        To specify a proxy
        Exemple: -p http://proxy:port/
-c <cookie_file>
--cookie <cookie_file>
        To use a cookie
-t <timeout>
--timeout <timeout>
        To fix the timeout (in seconds)
-a <login%password>
--auth <login%password>
        Set credentials for HTTP authentication
        Doesn't work with Python 2.4
-r <parameter_name>
--remove <parameter_name>
```

```
        Remove a parameter from URLs
-m <module>
--module <module>
        Use a predefined set of scan/attack options
        GET_ALL: only use GET request (no POST)
        GET_XSS: only XSS attacks with HTTP GET method
        POST_XSS: only XSS attacks with HTTP POST method
-u underline
        Use color to highlight vulnerables parameters in output
```

9.4 Paros:

Paros is used for web application security assessment. Paros is written in Java, and people generally used this tool to evaluate the security of their web sites and the applications that they provide on web site. It is free of charge, and using Paros's you can exploit and modified all HTTP and HTTPS data among client and server along with form fields and cookies. In brief the functionality of scanner is as below.

According to web site hierarchy server get scan, it checks for server misconfiguration. They add this feature because some URL paths can't be recognized and found by the crawler, and other automatic scanners are not able to do that. Basically to work this functions Paros navigate the site and rebuild the website hierarchy. Presently Paros do three types of server configuration checks. HTTP PUT , Directory indexable, and Obsolete file exist. Paros also provides log file, it create when all the HTTP request and reply pass through Paros. In log panel you can view back as request and reply format.

9.5 Pixy:

Pixy is the second tool that I found in web which is writtern in Java. Pixy does automatic scans for PHP 4 for the detection for SQL injection and XSS attacks. The major disadvantage of Pixy is that it only woks for PHP 4 and not for OOPHP 5. Pixy take whole PHP file as an input and produce a report that shows the possible vulnerability section in that PHP file along with some additional information to understand attack.

While SQL injection analysis Pixy divides result in three categories: untainted, weakly tainted, and strongly tainted. It also provide dependence graph and dependence value. Dependent value is nothing but the list of points in program on which the value of variables is depends.

9.6 Performance Evaluation of SQLiX with other commercial and open source tools:
Following tables are tabular representation of the performance evaluation among tools and the test cases which shows the performance of the each tool on corresponding web site.

Tools	Execution Time (Minutes)	No. of injections	UDF(user define function)	No. of type of attacks	Database supports	Language	GUI
SQLiX	2-3	300	YES	2	My SQL, Oracle, PSQL. MSsql, MS Acesses	Perl	Yes
Acunitix	25-30	__ __	NO	5	All above	-------	Yes
Sqlmap	4-5	41	NO	3	My SQL, Oracle, PSQL. MSsql	Python	No
Wapiti	7-8	XSS 90 SQL 40	NO	2	Except PSQL	Python	No
Paros	8-10	40	NO	2	--	Java	Yes
Pixy	4-5	--	NO	2	--	Java	Yes

Figure 13: Table shows performance evaluation for SQLiX with other tools.

Tools	Execution Time (Minutes)	Site
SQLiX	2-3	http://jagdishhalde.hostrator.com/indexacu.php
Acunitix	10-20	
Sqlmap	4-5	
Wapiti	7-8	
Paros	8-10	
Pixy	4-5	

Figure 14: Test case for http://jagdishhalde.hostrator.com/indexacu.php

Tools	Execution Time (Minutes)	Site
SQLiX	4-6	http://test.acunetix.com
Acunitix	25-30	
Sqlmap	7-8	
Wapiti	9-10	
Paros	4-6	
Pixy	25-30	

Figure 15: Test case for http://test.acunetix.com

Tools	Execution Time (Minutes)	Site
SQLiX	2-3	http://www.jeffgaroutte.com
Acunitix	8-10	
Sqlmap	4-5	
Wapiti	7-8	
Paros	8-10	
Pixy	4-5	

Figure 16: Test case for http://www.jeffgaroutte.com

Tools	Execution Time (Minutes)	Site
SQLiX	3-4	http://abhishek1984.zxq.net
Acunitix	10-12	
Sqlmap	4-5	
Wapiti	7-8	
Paros	8-10	
Pixy	4-5	

Figure 17: Test case for http://abhishek1984.zxq.net

Tools	Execution Time (Minutes)	Site
SQLiX	180-	http://inderweb.com
Acunitix	90-120	
Sqlmap	4-5/ Error	
Wapiti	N/A	
Paros	N/A	
Pixy	N/A	

Figure 18: Test case for http://inderweb.com

Tools	Execution Time (Minutes)	Site
SQLiX	180 -	http://www.surfindia.com
Acunitix	90-120/ ERROR	
Sqlmap	N/A	
Wapiti	N/A	
Paros	N/A	
Pixy	N/A	

Figure 19: Test case for http://www.surfindia.com

10.0   SQLiX Web Vulnerability test site:

I built a web site which is used to test SQLiX. This web site also provides information about basic SQL Injection attacks. I created two partition on the main web page, on one partition provides the component available on site and other part is used to show the back end of the site. The main intension behind this structure is that the third user can easily see how SQLiX tool injecting the different combination of given URL and trying to retrieve unauthorized information from the back end. I host this site on http:hostrator.com. To host first you need to register domain name and upload the all front end file as well as server scripts. I also import the database schemas and data that created on local host. Here is the link for hosted web site: http://jagdishhalde.hostrator.com/indexacu.php

Following are the few main screen shot of the web site.

Figure 20: SQLiX Web vulnerability site with home page SQLiX source site.

Figure 21: SQLiX Web vulnerability site with home page and back end user info table.

From this partition of web page any one can easily see the number of injection done by SQLiX on database. While scanning this particular web page injected entries related to database shown on right hand side.

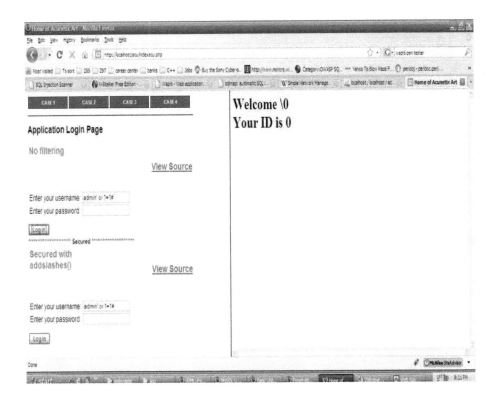

Figure 22: SQLiX Web vulnerability site showing basic SQL Injection attacks.

This web page gives some flavor of basic SQL Injection attacks. There are four cases that I tried to demo here. How SQL injection happens and what precaution we have to take while building web site.

11.0 Conclusion

Most of the web applications uses intermediate layer to accept a request from the user and retrieve sensitive information from the database. Most of the time they use scripting language to build intermediate layer. To breach security of database hacker often uses SQL injection techniques. Generally attacker tries to confuse the intermediate layer technology by reshaping the SQL queries. Perhaps, attacker will change the activities of the programmer for their benefits. A number of methods are used to avoid SQL injection attack at application level, but no feasible solution is available yet. This paper covered most powerful techniques used for SQL injection prevention. From my research it concludes that automated technique for preventing, detecting and logging the SQL injection attack in 'stored procedure' is commonly used and they are concrete method. Graph control method is also good for small databases systems.

SQLiX is one of the best web security scanner for finding SQL injection vulnerabilities from the web site though it is not sufficient to list other possible types of web attack. It is very efficient in terms of speed, insertion of number of injection and injecting your own function. You can juxtapose from the test cases represented above. Now this tool has GUI interface and HTTP POST method automatic form fill feature. GUI helps novice user to try all combination of attack without remembering all options, and HTTP Post method increase the number of injections injecting in to the database.

12.0 Future Work:

As future work, we want to evaluate the method using different web based application script with public domain to achieve great accuracy in SQL injection prevention approaches. Integrate SQLiX with nikto HTTP scanner, HTTP scanning proxies, and with metasploit. Also add feature to dump database and database schema.

References

1. Wei, K., Muthuprasanna, M., & Suraj Kothari. (2006, April 18). Preventing SQL injection attacks in stored procedures. Software Engineering IEEE Conference. Retrieved November 2, 2007, from http://ieeexplore.ieee.org

2. Thomas, Stephen, Williams, & Laurie. (2007, May 20). Using Automated Fix Generation to Secure SQL Statements. Software Engineering for Secure Systems IEEE CNF. Retrieved November 6, 2007, from http://ieeexplore.ieee.org

3. Merlo, Ettore, Letarte, Dominic, Antoniol & Giuliano. (2007 March 21). Automated Protection of PHP Applications Against SQL-injection Attacks. Software Maintenance and Reengineering, 11th European Conference IEEE CNF. Retrieved November 9, 2007, from http://ieeexplore.ieee.org

4. Wassermann Gary, Zhendong Su. (2007, June). Sound and precise analysis of web applications for injection vulnerabilities. ACM SIGPLAN conference on Programming language design and implementation PLDI, 42 (6). Retrieved November 7, 2007, from http://portal.acm.org

5. Friedl's Steve Unixwiz.net Tech Tips. (2007). SQL Injection Attacks by Example. Retrieved November 1, 2007, from http://www.unixwiz.net/techtips/sql-injection.html

6. Massachusetts Institute of Technology. Web Application S ecurity MIT Security Camp. Retrieved November 1, 2007, from http://web.mit.edu/net-security/Camp/2003/clambert-slides.pdf

7. Massachusetts Institute of Technology. Web Application Security MIT Security Camp. Retrieved November 1, 2007, from http://groups.csmail.mit.edu/pag/reading-group/wasserman07injection.pdf

8. Gregory T. Buehrer, Bruce W. Weide, and Paolo A. G. Sivilotti. The Ohio State University Columbus, OH 43210 Using Parse Tree Validation to Prevent SQL Injection Attacks. Retrieved January 2005, from http://portal.acm.org

9. Zhendong Su, Gary Wassermann. University of California, Davis. The Essence of Command Injection Attacks inWeb Applications. Retrieved January 11, 2006, from http://portal.acm.org

10. William G.J. Halfond, Alessandro Orso, and Panagiotis Manolios College of Computing – Georgia Institute of Technology. Using Positive Tainting and Syntax-Aware Evaluation to Counter SQL Injection Attacks. Retrieved November 11, 2006, from http://portal.acm.org

11. William G.J. Halfond and Alessandro Orso. College of Computing Georgia Institute of Technology. Preventing SQL Injection Attacks Using AMNESIA. Retrieved May 28, 2007, from http://portal.acm.org

12. José Fonseca, Marco Vieira, Henrique Madeira. CISUC, University of Coimbra Dep. of Informatics Engineering 3030 Coimbra – Portugal. Online Detection of Malicious Data Access Using DBMS Auditing. Retrieved March 20, 2008, from http://portal.acm.org

13. Frank S. Rietta 10630 Greenock Way Duluth, Georgia 30097. Application Layer Intrusion Detection for SQL Injection. Retrieved , Retrieved March 12, 2006, from http://portal.acm.org

14. Martin Bravenboer, Eelco Dolstra, Eelco Visser, Delft University of Technology The Netherlands. Preventing Injection Attacks with Syntax Embeddings A Host and Guest Language Independent Approach. Retrieved October 3, 2007, from http://portal.acm.org

15. Yuji Kosuga, Kenji Kono, Miyuki Hanaoka Department of Information and Computer Science Keio University. Sania: Syntactic and Semantic Analysis for Automated Testing against SQL Injection. Retrieved November 12, 2007, from IEEE Computer Society. http://ieeexplore.ieee.org

16. Benjamin Livshits and U´ lfar Erlingsson. Microsoft Research. Using Web Application Construction Frameworks to Protect Against Code Injection Attacks. Retrieved June 14, 2007, from http://ieeexplore.ieee.org

17. José Fonseca CISUC - Polithecnic Institute of Guarda, Marco Vieira, Henrique Madeira DEI/CISUC - University of Coimbra. Testing and comparing web vulnerability scanning tools for SQL injection and XSS attacks. Retrieved July 10, 2007, from http://ieeexplore.ieee.org

18.   Hal Berghel. Hijacking the Web Retrieved January 2, 2002, from http://portal.acm.org

19. Engin Kirda, Christopher Kruegel, Giovanni Vigna, and Nenad Jovanovic Technical University of Vienna. Noxes: A Client-Side Solution for Mitigating Cross-Site Scripting Attacks. Retrieved June 5, 2006, from http://portal.acm.org

20. http://www.owasp.org/index.php/Category:OWASP_SQLiX_Project
21. http://www.owasp.org/index.php/Category:OWASP_SQLiX_Project
22. http://search.cpan.org/~petdance/www-Mechanize-1.34/lib/www/Mechanize.pm
23. http://wapiti.sourceforge.net/
24. http://sqlmap.sourceforge.net/
25. http://www.acunetix.com/
26. http://en.wikipedia.org/wiki/Cross-site_scripting
27. http://en.wikipedia.org/wiki/SQL_injection
28. http://www.unixwiz.net/techtips/sql-injection.html
29. http://pixybox.seclab.tuwien.ac.at/pixy/index.php
30. http://www.parosproxy.ort/index.shtml

www.ingramcontent.com/pod-product-compliance
Lightning Source LLC
Chambersburg PA
CBHW051213050326
40689CB00008B/1296